The Least You Can Do Investment Strategy

TODD ALLEN

To the millions of good people out there with no savings, no investments, and no plans for how to retire with a full bank account. If you want to retire comfortably, I offer you here…The Least You Can Do. ☺

INTRODUCTION

The writing of this book came about because it dawned on me rather recently that no one in my life has any savings, investments, retirement strategies, or any plans to stop living off credit cards with wildly high interest rates. I am not exaggerating either. I am 35 years old and do not know anyone with a sensible savings or investment plan intact. Nobody. Zero. Zilch. I do not even know anyone who is thinking about starting one in the near future.

Frankly, I am not surprised, nor do I judge anyone for not saving and investing their money for later in life. For most people, the world of finance is much too dull and complicated to take even the slightest interest in it. Just the thought of anything financial often leaves one feeling completely overwhelmed. I think that is why so many smart, everyday people subscribe to the "do nothing" strategy. My hope is that I can encourage my family, friends, and fellow citizens to start taking care of their future finances – today.

So where do you begin if you detest all things money related, but do not want to retire in the poor-house? Many would suggest turning your money over to a professional money manager. In theory, this makes a lot of sense. Unfortunately, the statistics show gross immorality and very poor performance by "professional" money managers. I am very skeptical of anyone who charges large fees for something any person with average intelligence can do, even if they do not understand the world of finance.

"The least you can do investment strategy," as I call it, also turns out to be the most you can do. Meaning, you will get better results *(make more money)* than the majority of money managers, who charge hefty fees for their "help."

The strategy I am about to share with you is so simple that anyone can do it. It is not a get-rich-quick scheme, and it is far from a new idea. The concept has been recommended and proven by financial gurus for years. Warren Buffett, John Bogle, Burton Malkiel, and more all suggest similar advice for the average person. Then why read my book and not one by a financial genius? Because my book is short. Really short!

For those who have no interest in the details of money matters, there is no other book that provides such a simple, bare-bones explanation on how to implement a realistic, and proven retirement investment plan.

If you want to read billions of pages on finance, all dedicated to making money for retirement, by all means, go ahead. I read them. And I loved it. It was fascinating stuff. But if you are like most folks, you would prefer the CliffsNotes. Surprisingly, they have never been written. I suppose it is a little hard to charge much money for a book with less than 3,000 words. But here I am, writing it anyway.

In this very quick read, you will learn the absolute minimum you need to know about how to retire with a fat wallet. Consider this book the hyper-CliffsNotes on retirement investment. If you want to retire wealthy, this is truly the least you can do.

SAVE

The first step is, you have to save. There is no way around it. If you want to retire with enough money to support yourself, you must save money. **Saving means spending less than you earn**. Pretty simple. Get out of debt immediately. Pay off those credit cards, student loans, car payments, and everything else you owe outside of a mortgage. Going forward, stay out of debt. Then save at least 10 to 20 percent of your income each and every month.

Enjoy your life as you normally would, but find a few ways to save a little money while you do it: $20 a month is fine, $200 is good, $2,000 is better. Save anything and everything you can. Cut back on the daily coffee splurge. Pack a lunch once a week. Buy your clothes on sale. You already know how to do it, so do it! Saving is the only way to retire rich. Save money every day, every week, every month, and every year for the rest of your life.

INVEST YOUR SAVINGS

You want your savings to grow, right? Then that means you have to invest them. How do you do that? The easiest and most profitable way to invest your savings is to buy and own businesses. Productive businesses make money, and in return they pay that money back to their owners. You are an owner when you buy businesses. Pretty simple, so I will say it again. Be a business owner…make more money.

HOW DO I BUY AND OWN BUSINESSES?

The best way to buy a business with the least amount of effort *(lucky for you)* is to buy them by way of the stock market. That's right…the big, fat, scary stock market! In truth, it is not scary at all. The stock market is really just a list of businesses that are offered up for sale every Monday through Friday. Anyone can buy them. It is the same concept as your farmer's market. If you can buy a tomato at a market, you can buy a stock at a stock market. Stocks are businesses. Same thing. Buying shares in a stock means you will own a piece or portion of that business. You can buy into any company in the world if it is listed on the stock market.

For example: If you buy some stock or shares in Whole Foods, you are now a part-owner of Whole Foods. A portion of all the money Whole Foods earns will be paid back to you, the owner. The wealthier Whole Foods becomes, the wealthier you become.

WHERE DO I BUY STOCKS/BUSINESSES?

You can buy stocks or businesses right on your computer. It has never been easier. There are many companies that will assist you in becoming a business owner. All you have to do is set up an investment account with one of them. The experience is much like online banking. Vanguard, Fidelity, and TD Ameritrade are just a few of the choices out there. There are literally hundreds more. Vanguard *(vanguard.com)* charges the least amount of money in fees, so I believe they are the superior choice.

Open an account today by going to their website. Click on "open a new account" and follow the steps. You can select a taxable or non-taxable account. Select "taxable" for now. Non-taxable accounts have specific rules and income qualification requirements. A quick conversation with a tax accountant will clarify your non-taxable account options. You may also be able to buy stocks through your company's 401K plan. Buy your stocks and businesses in all of these types of accounts or just one. Whatever you decide, get started today!

WHAT STOCKS OR BUSINESSES DO I BUY?

Beats me! Frankly, picking individual stocks or businesses is not your game. Luckily, you do not have to pick. You are going to eliminate the entire guessing game by buying every business listed on the stock market. You are going to buy and own the world!

This is called diversification. The idea behind it is to limit risk. Rather than picking only one business or company to invest in and hoping it does well, you are going to spread your money out into many different businesses. Remember the old phrase, "Don't put all of your eggs in one basket"? Same idea applies here.

Over time, the value of all the businesses on the stock market continues to grow and grow. It may vary from year-to-year, but over the long haul, businesses will make more money and become more valuable. By owning all the businesses on the stock market, you will get the market return and your fair share of the profits.

Buying a piece of so many businesses is easier than you might think. It is accomplished by buying something called an **index fund**. Index funds are simply a one-stop-shop for buying all the businesses on the stock market. Thousands of businesses get pooled together into the index fund so you can buy them all in one convenient place. Much like a grocery store, where you can buy everything you need in one location, an index fund allows you to buy into every business on the stock market in one, easy transaction. When you buy shares in an index fund, you will be a shareholder or owner in the thousands of businesses within that fund.

Below are three index funds that hold and represent the majority of all the business value on the stock market. Think of all your favorite companies and more: Apple, Samsung, Disneyland, Hershey's, Tesla, etc. A huge portion of all the companies in the world are packaged right into the index fund for you to own.

1. Vanguard Total Stock Market Index Fund. Holds 3,698 different businesses from the United States. Represents 98 percent of all American businesses.

2. Vanguard Emerging Markets Index Fund. Holds 961 different businesses from China, Taiwan, Brazil, India, South Africa, Russia, Mexico, Malaysia, Indonesia, Poland, and more.

3. Vanguard Developed Markets Index Fund. Holds 1,370 different businesses from Japan, U.K., France, Germany, Switzerland, Australia, Korea, Spain, Hong Kong, Sweden, Italy, and more.

You can buy only the first index fund, which holds most of the businesses in the United States, or you can buy all three, in equal amounts, and you will own businesses from across the world. Either choice is fine. You do not need to own more than three index funds to be well diversified and to accomplish your goal – retiring with plenty of money.

These are just three examples of index funds that cover a huge cross-section of global business. There are others. However, these three funds charge some of the lowest operating fees out there, meaning more money for you. Buying index funds with the lowest fee or cost structure is important.

For example: If you have the choice between using two ATM machines, where one charges a $2 fee and the other charges a $5 fee, which one are you going to choose? You get it. It is just like in everyday life – keep your expenses low!

When you buy shares in these three index funds you will become a part-owner in the thousands of businesses in the United States and from around the world. As an owner, you are now entitled to a portion of every dollar these businesses earn. When these businesses earn more money, they become more valuable, and so will your piece of the ownership.

WALK ME THROUGH THE BUYING PROCESS

To buy shares or ownership in these index funds, you simply log into your investment account. Select "buy stocks." Type in the name of the index fund you want to buy. The price listed will be for one share.

For example: If the price is $50 for one share and you have $100 in your account, you can buy two shares. Select "confirm buy" and within minutes you will be a business owner. The goal here is to buy as many shares as you can. The bigger your ownership stake, the more money your businesses will earn for you.

HOW OFTEN DO I BUY?

Buy consistently every month or every year for the rest of your life. Never stop buying. Never stop investing. The stock market will go up and it will go down. The price to purchase your index funds or businesses will fluctuate every day. All kinds of "experts" will have lots to say to about it. Do not pay any attention to them. Just keep buying and **do not sell** because you are building up your ownership in business. This takes years.

When the stock market goes down, celebrate! Everything is on sale. Buy more because you are getting more for less. When the stock market goes up, do not get too excited. Ignore the daily noise or tips from television, newspapers and neighbors. Just keep buying until you are old. How old is old? Sixty-five, seventy-five, seconds before death? That is for you to decide. Buy. Buy. Buy. Keep buying more shares and do not stop.

DIVIDENDS

Sometimes the businesses you own through the index funds will pay you cash. These payments are called dividends. Dividends get deposited right into your investment account. Typically, this happens four times a year. Consider it a birthday present that comes every three months. It is really just business doing what it is supposed to do: paying its owners for being owners.

When you get these little cash gifts, use the money to increase your ownership stake. Do not spend it. Re-invest it. Buy more shares in the businesses you already own by buying more shares in the index funds. Set up your investment accounts so dividends get automatically re-invested for you. This way you do not even have to think about it.

DO I EVER SELL?

The short answer is no. You want to focus on the buying. Building up substantial ownership in businesses requires that you consistently buy for a very long time. For the best results, your shares in the index funds should only be sold when you can comfortably live off what you have accumulated. It takes years to get to this point. Think twenty or thirty years of buying before you even consider selling anything.

Owning businesses for the long term will reap the best rewards. Time is truly the best partner a business owner can have. After all the years of saving and investing, you will be pleasantly surprised by how much money your ownership in businesses is now worth. The amount may boggle your mind!

Selling your shares in index funds is similar to selling any business. You need to find a buyer. Lucky for you, the stock market has millions of buyers and sellers every day. When it comes time for you to sell, you will simply select the "sell" option in your investment account. Type in how many shares of your index funds you want to sell. Buyers from around the world will purchase your shares in a matter of minutes. For now, though, concentrate on the buying.

IS THAT IT?

Yep! This is really all you have to do to ensure that you have lots of money for later in life. It is not complicated. Do you want to work at Walmart when you are sixty-five? No! Then save and invest your money every month, starting today. The longer you save, invest and retain ownership in businesses, the more money you will end up with. This is truly the least you can do to make the most amount of money.

Perhaps now you want to learn more about all things financial? If so, there are years of reading waiting for you at your local library. The good books ultimately say exactly what you have just read – they just take longer to get to the point. These books do offer some valuable insights into many of the specifics of financial planning, but if you want to retire rich, while completely ignoring or checking out from all of the details, then "The Least You Can Do Investment Strategy" will treat you just fine.

Consistently buying businesses, over a long period of time, through very low-cost index funds that cover a wide spectrum of countries and industries will ensure you get better results than the majority of investors and money managers. You can do this. Begin today. It is the least you can do for your future self!

HOW ABOUT A QUICK RECAP?

- Get out of debt and stay out of debt.

- Save money every month – at least 10 to 20 percent of your income.

- Saving money means spending less than you earn.

- Open an investment account at vanguard.com or another online broker.

- The investment company you select should have low or zero account costs.

- Open a taxable account.

- Consult a tax accountant about your non-taxable account options.

- Transfer your savings into your investment account(s) every month.

- **Consistently buy index funds that hold or represent almost all of the businesses in the United States or the world.**

- Buying one to three index funds is sufficient. You do not need more.

- Make sure your index funds have a very low fee structure.

- Set up your account so dividends are reinvested automatically.

- Do not worry about stock market fluctuations or negative news.

- Over time, save more money!

- Keep buying businesses and do not stop!

- Twenty or thirty years from now, take a look at your account balance.

- Prepare to be shocked at how much your ownership is worth.

- Sell only when you can comfortably live off what you have accumulated.

NOTES

How could you get out of debt?

- Consolidate your credit cards into one card with a lower interest rate.
- Make debt payments twice a month.
- Apply for debt forgiveness on student loans.

Write down more of your own ideas here:

NOTES

How could you save more?

- Earn more money.
- Ask for a promotion or a raise.
- Get a new job.
- Cut back on expenses like eating out.
- Could you move to a cheaper house?

Write down more of your own ideas here:

NOTES

What kind of lifestyle do you want in retirement?

- How much will this cost?
- How much do you have to save and invest to achieve this?

Write down more of your own ideas here:

NOTES

How much money could you realistically save every month, starting today?

NOTES

DISCLAIMER

This book claims no guarantee of financial success. The future is unknown. But two things are for certain: Doing nothing will guarantee you get nothing in return, and handing your savings over to a money manager will cost you a big chunk of your own hard-earned dough. This book is the minimalist's approach to investing. There are many additional factors you may wish to learn about. If so, read everything you can. ☺

AUTHOR

Todd Allen is an investor, among other things. He buys real estate, index funds, stocks, and private businesses. He is an avid reader on the topic of investment. He lives in Santa Monica, California with his wife and two children. If you have questions about investing for retirement please email him at toddcallen@gmail.com and he will respond as quickly as possible.